Siobhan's Journey

Siobhan's Journey

A Belfast Girl Visits the United States

Barbara Beirne

Carolrhoda Books, Inc./Minneapolis

This book is dedicated to Denis and Miriam Mulcahy, who in 1975 invited six children from Belfast to Greenwood Lake, New York, for a summer holiday. This compassionate gesture initiated Project Children, an organization which now invites over 900 children to the United States from Belfast each summer. Denis and Miriam continue to be the heart and soul of Project Children.

Some of the words and phrases that Siobhan uses may be unfamiliar. They are explained in the glossary on page 48.

Siobhan's name is pronounced shuh-VAHN.

LIBRARY OF CONGRESS CATALOGING-IN-PUBLICATION DATA

Beirne, Barbara.
  Siobhan's journey / Barbara Beirne.
    p.   cm.
  Summary: Describes the experiences of ten-year-old Siobhan McNulty, a girl from Northern Ireland who spent six weeks with a New Jersey family as a part of Project Children.
  ISBN 0-87614-728-7
  1. McNulty, Siobhan—Juvenile literature. 2. Intercultural communication—New Jersey—Juvenile literature. 3. Exchange of persons programs, British—New Jersey—Juvenile literature. 4. Irish—New Jersey—Biography—Juvenile literature. 5. Children—Northern Ireland—Biography—Juvenile literature. [1. Exchange of persons programs. 2. McNulty, Siobhan.] I. Title.
F145.I6M384   1993
917.4904'43—dc20
[B]   91-44815
                                                                     CIP
                                                                      AC

Manufactured in the United States of America

1 2 3 4 5 6 98 97 96 95 94 93

Northern Ireland and the Troubles

Northern Ireland is a small country located in the northeast corner of the island of Ireland. This country is part of the United Kingdom, which also includes England, Scotland, and Wales. The larger portion of this island is the Republic of Ireland, which is governed independently.

The majority of the citizens of Northern Ireland are Protestant, and most believe their country should maintain its ties to England and the rest of the United Kingdom. Many Catholic citizens of Northern Ireland, along with the majority of the people living in the Republic of Ireland (who are also Catholic), feel Northern Ireland should be part of the Republic of Ireland.

The history of bitter conflicts between these countries is long and complicated. The struggles are not simply about religious differences but also about civil liberties and justice. All of the problems are referred to as "the Troubles."

My name is Siobhan McNulty, and I live in Belfast, Northern Ireland. I live in a Catholic section of the city called Ardoyne.

My best friend is Jamie Alexander. We love to skateboard and babysit for my nephew Ciaran.

This is going to be a very special summer for me. Every summer, hundreds of children from Northern Ireland are invited to travel to America for a summer holiday. This year, I was selected to make the journey along with 10 other children from my school. I'll have to leave my family. I have 10 brothers and sisters, but they don't all live at home.

I'll travel with an organization called Project Children. Almost everyone in Belfast has heard of this grand organization. Project Children has arranged for Catholic and Protestant children from Northern Ireland to visit America since 1975. My teacher said that this year, 902 children will be going on a summer holiday.

I'm not certain how you get chosen, but it seems most of the children selected live in cities and towns like Belfast, Derry, and Newry, where there's a lot of trouble. In my country, many of the Catholics and Protestants don't get along. There's a lot of fighting, and children have been hurt by things like petrol bombs and plastic bullets. Sometimes there are bomb scares in my neighborhood. It's really frightening, don't you know.

Project Children pays for the trip, and they select a family for each child to visit. My mum tells me that the people in America who are part of Project Children work really hard to make enough money to pay for the hundreds of airplane tickets. All year long they have events like dances, bake sales, and raffles to earn the money. I only have to pay for my passport.

The American family that I'll visit are called the Farrells. They have five children. What's really lovely is that they have a daughter, Lauren, who's 10 years old. That's just how old I am. Lauren and I have written letters to each other.

Lauren said in her letter that she likes to swim and play games. Since I like sports and games, I'm sure we'll have good fun together. The Farrells sound like a grand family. I'll live at their house in New Jersey for six weeks.

Dear Siobhan,

My name is Lauren Farell. I am ten years old. I have three brothers and [a] sister, Michael 13, [Jo...] Kevin 6 and Heather [1]. I like to play soccer a[nd] softball. I have a b[rown] cocker-spaniel, her [name] is Maggie. I can't [wait] for the summer [so] [I'll] get to meet you [so] we can go to the beac[h]. [The] beach is fun because [you] can go swimming [in the] ocean and lay out [and get] a tan. I can't wait to see y[ou].

From,
Lauren Farell

11

The day before my trip is a busy one. Mum and I have to make certain all my clothes are ready and packed. I know exactly what kinds of clothes to take on my trip, because my sister Phyllis and my brother Tony have been to America. Phyllis says that it's really warm in America in the summer, so I bring all my lightest shirts and trousers. Mum buys me a gorgeous purple dress to wear the day of the trip.

All my friends and neighbors stop over to say good-bye and wish me luck. Mr. Watt, who lives next door, reminds me not to forget my passport.

I've never been away before, and it's really hard saying good-bye. I feel scared. Suddenly, my stomach starts to tremble, and I wonder if going to America is a good idea. My mother knows I'm upset. When she tucks me into bed, Mum tells me not to feel sad. I ask if everyone will miss me. "Aye, we'll miss you very much, Siobhan, but you'll learn so much in America, and most important, I know you'll be safe." Mum worries a lot about the Troubles.

The next morning, Mum brings me to the airport. I have to wear a plastic card with the number 248 on it. Each child and his or her American family have been assigned the same number. My number will make it easier for my family to find me at the massive airport in New York. At Belfast Airport, I can tell that the other children are feeling as nervous as I am. It's hard not to cry when I kiss Mum good-bye.

Soon after we find our seats on the huge 747 jet, all the children start talking about America. Everyone says it's a lovely place, and pretty soon, I start to feel better about my journey. My friend Edele is visiting her American family for the second year, and she tells me that she played outside all last summer and never saw any soldiers patrolling the streets. She didn't even hear of one bomb exploding all summer long.

The plane ride is brilliant. Would you believe it—we are served two meals and watch two movies! I even get to play cards and listen to music on a headset. Three of my friends are going to New York; one friend will visit Pennsylvania, and one is going to a place called Ohio. Project Children sends children to 16 states.

In only 6 hours and 10 minutes, we fly from Belfast to New York City. When the captain tells us to fasten our seat belts for landing, thoughts start to run through my brain. Will I like America? Will the Farrells like me? Will I be homesick? Will the airplane land safely? At the very moment that I'm thinking all this, the wheels of the jet touch the runway, and we come to a gentle stop on American soil.

Everyone peers out the windows of the plane to get their first glimpse of America. We see hundreds and hundreds of people have come to greet us. The people are smiling, and many have signs that say, "WELCOME." America seems a very friendly place.

Dr. and Mrs. Farrell are at the airport with three of their children—Lauren, Tommy, and Kevin. They all wave and cheer like they've known me forever. When I meet Dr. and Mrs. Farrell they give me a hug and then tell me they'd like me to call them by their first names—Paul and Karen. I hope I can remember that because in my country, I don't call many adults by their first names. Then they introduce me to everyone, including Lauren's friend Bryn. Can you believe it, they even give me flowers. This greeting is a real smasher, don't you know.

On the trip from the airport to New Jersey, I feel quite shy. It's really very difficult when you don't know anyone. I can tell right away, though, that Lauren and I are going to be friends. Lauren talks and laughs a lot. I know she's trying to make me feel comfortable.

As we drive along, I look out the car window. We're on a busy motorway. There are thousands of cars, and they all seem to be speeding and honking their horns. Some of the cars are massive. I wonder to myself how people can afford the petrol for these huge motorcars. And I wonder too why everyone is in such a hurry. Where is everyone going?

We walk to a pretty little town called Spring Lake, which is right next to Wall Township. There are lots of shops, and I find some postcards to send home. I have to borrow American money from Lauren. All the money I have is the money used in Northern Ireland. My pounds, shillings and pence will have to be exchanged at the bank for dollars, quarters, and pennies. The postcards seem very dear (or expensive, as Americans say). But maybe that's because I'm not used to paying in dollars. My sister Phyllis told me that $1.00 is about the same as 60 pence.

Lauren and I then decide to stop at a shop for a wee meal. The waitress politely gives me a menu, but when I try to read it I can't believe my eyes. There's hardly a thing on the menu that's recognizable. I don't know what to order. "What are you going to have, Lauren?"

"I guess I'll have french fries and a soda," Lauren says. I decide to order the same thing—just hoping that I'll like whatever it is.

When our food arrives, I find it's just what I wanted. In Belfast, soda is called "lemonade" and french fries are called "chips." Americans may speak the same language as I do, but it isn't always going to be easy to understand them. Lauren says that she has a little trouble understanding me, too.

For the first few days, I feel a little homesick, but as each day passes I'm a bit more comfortable and less shy. All the Farrells treat me like I'm a member of the family.

Lauren and I enjoy doing the same things. Almost every day, we ride our bicycles to the beach. The Farrells' house is only a wee bike ride to the Atlantic Ocean.

My house in Belfast is close to the Irish Sea, which is part of the Atlantic Ocean too. The coastline is gorgeous in Northern Ireland, but the water is very cold. We swim indoors at a leisure center. Lauren's brother Tommy says he's never heard of a leisure center. He says that in the United States indoor swimming pools are usually in health clubs or recreation centers. It's good fun to swim outdoors. There's a lovely breeze on the beach that comes in from the sea.

Lauren and I love to sunbathe. It would be brilliant to get a suntan. The only people who are tan in Belfast are the ones who've been on holiday, because there are so many rain showers during the summer.

I notice that everywhere we go people are talking about a special holiday—the Fourth of July. This day is just like any other in Northern Ireland. Lauren says that it's the birthday of the United States of America, so every year there's a big celebration.

When the Fourth of July arrives, we get up early and go to a big parade. There are lots of policemen at the parade, but they seem very friendly. It's grand that the police in America don't carry rifles. After the parade, there's a carnival with amusements and rides. Our favorite ride is the bumper cars. You bump into everyone, even people you don't know. We can't stop laughing.

The Fourth of July is a wonderful day. It's surprising to see people of all different religions celebrate the same holiday. People in America say that someday everyone in my country will celebrate the same holiday, but I don't think so. In Belfast, the Protestants parade on July 12th. It's the anniversary of the Battle of the Boyne, when William of Orange, a Protestant English king, defeated James II, who was Catholic. In August, the Catholics march to remember a time when many Catholics were put in prison without a trial.

When it gets dark on the Fourth of July, we go to see the fireworks. Karen and Paul warn me about the loud explosions so I won't be scared, but I still don't like this part of the day. The fireworks are pretty, but the noises are frightening.

I'm really lucky because my family writes to me a lot. It's grand to hear from them, but I must admit, the letters make me feel a wee homesick.

Lauren and I spend our evenings in the backyard. The kids from the neighborhood come over and play football, which in America is called soccer. Sometimes we just swing on a rope. Lauren's friends are just like my friends at home in many ways, but not all our games are the same. I teach Lauren and Bryn a game we play in Belfast. It's called "two balls" because you play it with two balls, one in each hand. You throw one ball at a wall with your right hand and then throw the other ball at the wall with your left hand. The object is to see how long you can throw the balls without dropping one. It's not as easy as it sounds.

Some nights we sit outdoors after it gets dark and talk about life in America and Northern Ireland. I've learned that both our countries have problems. One of my biggest surprises about America is that there are a lot of homeless people. I thought everyone in America was rich. All the Americans we see on the telly in Belfast seem rich.

Lauren asks me why I don't have any Protestant friends. I tell her it's just the way it is.

Americans seem to love to eat outdoors, and they have lots of outdoor parties called picnics. At home we don't have many picnics because of the weather. My favorite picnic of the summer is held at the Allaire State Park.

It's a Project Children picnic. All of the children from Northern Ireland and their American families from Monmouth County, New Jersey, are invited.

Keri McCusker, a girl who attends the same school as I do, is at the picnic, but the other children from Northern Ireland are strangers. They're from Derry, Strabane, Larne, Lurgan, and Enniskillen. I knew I'd meet lots of Americans this summer, but I never realized I'd meet so many kids from my own country. Keith Browne from Larne is really friendly and funny. What a surprise when I find out he's Protestant. I wonder what my friends at home will think when I tell them I met a Protestant and he was really all right.

All afternoon we eat and play games. The kids from Northern Ireland aren't very good at baseball, but we sure know how to play soccer. In one part of the park there's an historic village. Everything looks just the way it did in the 1830s. In fact, the people who show us around the buildings all wear old-fashioned clothes. It's really interesting, especially the blacksmith's shop. Allaire Village looks very much like the Ulster-American Folk Park in Omagh, County Tyrone. My school visited this park just last year. There were thatched cottages, and people in costumes showed us how to use a spinning wheel.

We don't go to parties all the time. The adults work very hard. Karen is a school nurse during the school year, and during the summer she's very busy around the house. All of the kids have jobs as well.

Lauren and I like it best when our job is to make the sweet. Karen helps us and so does Kevin. Our cakes often don't look great, but the Farrells say that the only thing that matters is how the cake tastes.

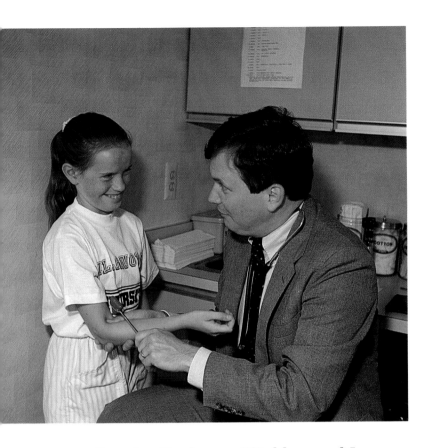

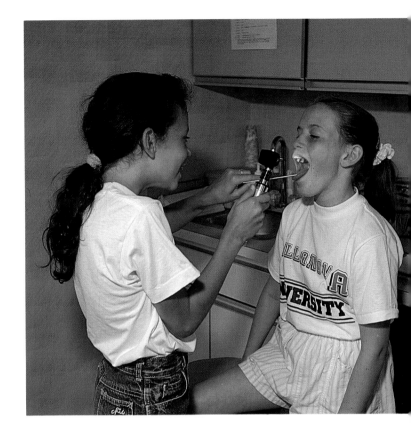

One day Paul says, "Siobhan and Lauren, why don't you come to work with me?" I'm really surprised, because Paul is a children's doctor. I'm afraid we'll have to sit in his waiting room with a lot of sick babies. Much to my surprise, it wasn't boring at all. Paul's office looks just like my doctor's surgery at home. He even has a little rubber hammer to check children's reflexes that looks just like my doctor's hammer. The best part is that Paul lets us touch some of his instruments. Lauren and I take turns using a tongue blade and torch to check each other's throats. Lauren says she can see my tonsils. Lauren wants to be a veterinarian when she grows up. She thinks taking care of sick animals would be even better than taking care of sick people. I'm not certain what I want to be. Maybe I'll be a nurse like Karen.

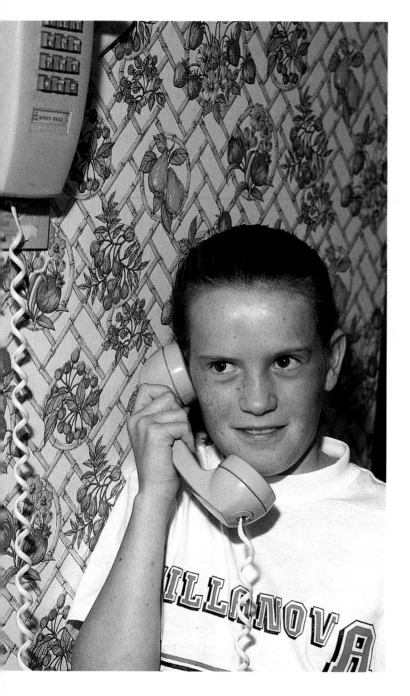

A day I'll never forget is my 11th birthday, on July 20th. At breakfast everyone sings "Happy Birthday." Karen and Paul have a big surprise for me. "Would you like to telephone your family?" Paul asks.

"Aye, indeed I would!"

Paul dials the telephone number. My family doesn't have a telephone, so we have to ring our neighbors, the Watts. Mrs. Watt answers the phone and then runs to my house to get my family. I can hear everyone shouting, "Hurry, hurry! It's Siobhan from America." My mother, two sisters, and one brother are home, and they take turns getting on the telephone. I'm happy to hear they are all well and safe. Being able to talk to my family is a wonderful birthday present. And don't you know, they sounded just like they were right next door.

In the afternoon, we drive to a beautiful peach orchard where the customers are allowed to pick their own peaches. I've never done this before. I also love taking motor trips, because I don't have a chance to travel very often at home. My brother Tony has a car, but he needs it for work. Sometimes my mum and I take bus trips with our church, but I've never had a chance to pick fruit before. There are so many peaches on the trees that our buckets are full in a very short time. A man who works on the farm weighs our buckets. We pay him and then get to take our peaches home.

At teatime, the Farrells have a party for me. Karen fixes my very favorite meal, which is shepherd's pie—ground beef and mashed potatoes mixed together. The Farrells don't seem to love this meal, but I do. It's really good with red sauce. For sweet, there's a birthday cake made of ice cream, and some lovely gifts. Karen and Paul give me a watch that's just like Lauren's. The children give me a gorgeous pink shirt. On the shirt are printed the words, "Someone in New Jersey Loves Me." The whole day is really great!

The final two weeks in America fly by. Then, before it seems possible, it's time to start thinking about going home. Heather takes me shopping for gifts. I try to find a wee gift for everyone in my family. I find the perfect gift for my mum. It's a beautiful mug that she can use when she drinks tea. It's white with gold trim, and on the front of the mug it says, "Greetings from the U.S.A." It's perfect. For my brothers I buy some sweets, and I find some nice-looking barrettes for my sisters' hair.

The day before I leave, we go visit the Statue of Liberty. At home I've heard many people tell stories about how much this amazing statue meant to their relatives who emigrated to America. My teacher said that many people from Northern Ireland emigrated to America because they heard that it was possible to have religious freedom there, and if you worked hard, you could make a lot of money. People had to save their money for months and months to pay for their ticket. But that wasn't the end of their troubles. The ocean was often very rough, and many passengers got sick. In fact, a lot of people died. When the ship finally sailed into the New York harbor, and the immigrants saw the Statue of Liberty, they knew their journey was over and their dream had come true.

There is a special boat that takes us to Liberty Island, where the statue is located. It sails us right past the New York City skyline. All I can see are millions of massive buildings all lined up on a wee bit of land. I wonder why Americans want everything to be so close together. It's amazing that the heavy buildings don't sink into the Hudson River. I tell Lauren that the tallest building in Belfast is a big insurance building in city center. It's probably about 20 stories high. I used to think that was really something!

As we move closer to Liberty Island, we lean over the side of the boat to see who will catch the first glimpse of the Statue of Liberty. Tommy says, "This is just what the immigrants did on their journey to America a long time ago." When I finally see the statue, it's so gorgeous it takes my breath away. I can't wait to tell my teacher about it.

Liberty Island is crowded with hundreds of people. The visitors look like they're from all over the world. We wait in line to walk to the crown. The climb up is long and hot. The stairs become narrow as you reach the top, but even Kevin, who's only five years old, doesn't get discouraged. The view from the crown makes you forget about the long climb. It's absolutely brilliant! We look at the New York skyline again, but now the buildings look like toys.

When we get back to Wall Township, Lauren and I go up to our room. We're feeling really sad, because we know tomorrow I'll be going home. We won't see each other for a long time, but we are *definitely* going to see each other again. The Farrells have written to my mother to ask her if I can visit next summer. Lauren says sometime she's coming to visit me in Belfast. She wants to see the city where I live and meet my family.

When the time comes to leave, Paul takes one last photo of me with Heather, Michael, Lauren, Tommy, and Kevin. I'm feeling all mixed up. I'm really sad about leaving the Farrells, but I'm also excited and happy about going home. I've really missed my family and friends. It will be great to sleep in my own bed again and eat one of my mum's delicious meals.

This has been the most wonderful summer of my life. I've had a grand journey to the U.S.A., and I've learned that there are lots of people who care about me and my country. The hundreds of people who volunteer with Project Children work with this organization because they don't want children— either Catholic or Protestant—to get hurt in Northern Ireland. It's nice to know that there are so many people who care.

I've also learned that kids are kids. It doesn't matter what country they live in or what religion they are. In fact, there are many religions in America, and people seem to get along. Perhaps I can hope that some-day people will live more peacefully in my lovely country.

Glossary

aye: yes

brilliant: great, fun

chips: french fries

dear: expensive

football: soccer. In Northern Ireland, the type of football played in the United States is called American football.

gardens: yards (but what Americans call gardens are also called gardens in Northern Ireland)

motorway: highway or freeway

mum: nickname for mother

peace line: a high fence put up between Catholic and Protestant neighborhoods in some sections of Northern Ireland's cities

petrol: gasoline

porridge: oatmeal

red sauce: ketchup

ring: to call on the telephone

a smasher: great, wonderful

shepherd's pie: seasoned ground beef covered by a layer of mashed potatoes

surgery: in Northern Ireland, this means a doctor's office as well as the act of operating on someone.

sweet: dessert

teatime: dinnertime

telly: television

torch: flashlight

wee: small, little